MW00897351

HE IS

Jesus, The Man Without Equal

SIGNATURE SERIES

NewLife
PUBLICATIONS

He Is: Jesus, The Man Without Equal

Published by
NewLife Publications
375 Highway 74 South, Suite A
Peachtree City, GA 30269

Design and production by Genesis Group

Printed in the United States of America

Unless otherwise indicated, all Scripture references are from the *New International Version*, © 1973, 1978, 1984 by the International Bible Society. Published by Zondervan Bible Publishers, Grand Rapids, Michigan.

Scripture quotations designated TLB are from *The Living Bible*, © 1971 by Tyndale House Publishers, Wheaton, Illinois.

Scripture quotations designated NKJ are from the *New King James* version, © 1979, 1980, 1982 by Thomas Nelson Inc., Publishers, Nashville, Tennessee.

Scripture quotations designated Phillips are from The *Letters to Young Churches*, a translation of the New Testament Epistles, © 1947 by The MacMillan Company, New York, New York.

CONTENTS

This book, part of the Bill Bright *Signature Series*, is a condensation of *A Man without Equal*, which was published in 1992.

As Members of
Global Founding Partners

the following families are helping to fulfill the Great Commission through helping to train Millions of Pastors around the world.

Bill and Christie Heavener and Family
Ed and Edye Haddock and Family
Stuart and Debbie Sue Irby and Family

FOREWORD

OVER THE PAST twenty years, countless reporters and interviewers have asked me what the secret has been to the success of the *"JESUS"* film. Without question, my answer has always been: "The power is in the message." That message is the love and forgiveness of the greatest person who ever lived—Jesus of Nazareth.

For more than fifty years, Bill Bright continually pointed everyone who would listen to Jesus, the Author and Giver of Life Eternal.

Many years ago, God gave Bill Bright a vision to produce a film on the life of Christ. Recognizing that the majority of the world's population cannot read, a film seemed the best way to present Christ to the multitudes. The completion of that film, *"JESUS,"* and its use by many mission organizations worldwide is a fulfillment of that dream.

Under Bill's gracious leadership, I took the responsibility to help get the film translated into other languages and distributed in every country of the world. One day I returned from a trip to Africa where we had just completed the premiere of a new language translation for the Masaai people of Kenya. I was at Warner Brothers Studio for the day, and I decided to stop in to see several of the top executives and present them with Masaai warrior spears that I brought back with me. When I asked to see them, a secretary said, "They're all in the conference room meeting with the lawyers. There's a writers' strike on. You might as well go in though; they're not getting anything done."

As I walked in with my spears, one of the lawyers remarked, "Finally, a solution to the writers' strike!" We laughed, and talked about how the *"JESUS"* film was the first film distributed by Warner Brothers to ever be released in the jungles of the Masaai warriors of Africa.

Then one of the executives asked, "What would have happened if we had shown them the old action film *Dirty Harry*? Would they have become his follower?"

I answered, "The people in that area of the world have never seen a film before. They probably would have enjoyed the action, but their lives would not have been changed."

It is only the words of Jesus Christ that change lives. For over 2,000 years they have remained the most powerful, captivating, inspiring words that have ever been uttered. They can absolutely transform an individual's life—because Jesus can bring peace to a world of chaos. And as I looked around the room I saw these men, hardened from the dog-eat-dog competition of the movie business, solemnly nodding their heads. There is something so soothing and so promising about the words of Jesus that sparks of hope are kindled whenever His name is lifted up.

The pages of this book tell you much about the Man without equal, Jesus Christ. The beauty of the message of who He is cannot be fully appreciated until you see the reality of a relationship with Him lived out in the lives of His followers. Bill Bright is a devout follower of Jesus Christ, and you are certain to sense his passion for the Man in this book.

PAUL ESHLEMAN

one

WHY DOES IT MATTER?

THE DISTINGUISHED professor and dean of a famous theological seminary appeared to be in profound thought as we entered his cluttered study. Thousands of books filled the shelves that lined his office.

I was invited to visit this internationally known scholar by a friend who had been his student at the seminary. My friend, the associate pastor of a historic local church, introduced me. "This is Bill Bright, president of Campus Crusade for Christ. He works with students and professors all over the world."

Politely waving us to sit down, the professor asked curiously, "Mr. Bright, when you talk to students about becoming a Christian, what do you tell them?"

Not wanting to appear shallow and simplistic to such a learned man, I weighed my words carefully. Before I could reply, the professor furrowed his brows and asked a second question: "Better still, what would you tell me? I would like to become a Christian."

Now I was really puzzled and even more cautious. Why would a world-famous scholar and theologian, the dean of one of the most prestigious seminaries in the world, ask a total stranger to help him become a Christian?

"Before you answer my question," he interjected, "let me give you the background of my spiritual quest."

With transparent honesty, he explained that his father was a famous scholar who denied the deity of Jesus of Nazareth. His father and his teachings profoundly influenced his own views—that Jesus was a great and good man, but not the Son of God.

"But my heart was never satisfied," he confessed. "I had no peace. Then a couple of years ago, I began my own research in earnest. I had to know the truth."

He paused thoughtfully, then related how he had studied with new interest the passages in the Bible concerning Jesus. He also had searched the writings and biographies of great Christian leaders of the centuries. "Now I am absolutely persuaded that Jesus is more than a great leader and teacher. He is the Son of God, the Savior of men!"

The professor told us that he believed this intellectually, but did not know Jesus as Augustine, Martin Luther, John Wesley, and others knew Him. "I want to know Him personally as they did. Can you help me?"

My heart leaped for joy. Using a spare piece of paper on the professor's desk, I drew a circle on it. "This represents your life," I explained. In the circle I drew a throne, and on the throne I wrote the letter "S" for self. Pausing, I pointed to the "S."

"To become a Christian, you must receive Jesus Christ as your Savior from sin. To live a full, abundant life, you must surrender the control of your life to Him by making Him your Lord and Master..."

We were interrupted by a knock on the door. It opened slightly, and a voice said, "Your next appointment is here, Professor."

At the professor's insistence, my friend and I returned two days later to continue our conversation. He greeted us warmly and took us into an office with no telephones.

Locking the door behind us, he spoke enthusiastically. "I went to church early this morning to take communion to prepare my heart for your coming. I have been waiting for you. Can you help me? I want to know Jesus as my personal Savior."

My pastor friend, quiet until now, spoke up skeptically. "Professor, are you sure you understand what you are saying? Do you truly believe that Jesus is the Son of God, the only Savior of men?"

The professor sighed, a bit impatient. "I have wrestled with these intellectual questions all of my life and have found no answers." Turning to me, he continued. "After several years of personal research, I am now absolutely convinced that Jesus is the Son of God. And I am fully persuaded that no honest person who is willing to consider the overwhelming evidence proving the deity of Jesus Christ can deny that He is the Son of God. Now, will you pray for me?"

> *I am fully persuaded that no honest person who is willing to consider the evidence can deny that Jesus is the Son of God.*

First I prayed; then he prayed; and my friend prayed. That day this man of international renown received Jesus Christ as his Savior by faith, in the spirit of a little child. Later I was reminded of the words of Jesus: "Unless you turn to God from your sins and become as little children, you will never get into the Kingdom of Heaven" (Matthew 18:3, TLB).

It was a historic, life-changing experience for this great man and an unforgettable day for my friend and me. The professor's whole life was transformed. His teachings and philosophy of life were revolutionized.

Every day more and more people are taking a look—and some, a second one—at the historical person of Jesus of Nazareth. Men and women everywhere are getting excited about Him.

My wife, Vonette, and I, along with thousands of our associates, have personally observed this same hunger for Jesus in countries around the world. On university campuses, in hundreds of metropolitan centers, in towns, villages, and primitive or remote areas, we have witnessed this hunger for Jesus Christ.

This is evidenced by the millions of people who have flocked to see the "*JESUS*" film.[1] Wherever the film is shown, people from all walks of life gather to learn more about Jesus. Tens of millions have responded to the invitation to make Him their Savior and Lord.

In the early 1990s, we participated in three *"JESUS"* film premieres under prestigious sponsorship in Moscow, Leningrad, and Kiev. In each case, we showed the film to top government officials—including mayors and ministers of education, justice, and finance—as well as intellectuals and other leaders. Hundreds of actors, actresses, producers, directors, writers, and other dignitaries in the filmmakers' union also viewed the film and responded enthusiastically, with many receiving Christ.

We also heard Kalevi Lehtinen, one of Europe's leading Christian spokesmen and a Campus Crusade for Christ staff evangelist, speak about Jesus to approximately 75,000 people. At three separate meetings in Leningrad, he spoke to audiences of more than 25,000, and an estimated seventy million viewed the final meeting on television. An estimated 50 to 80 percent of those hearing his messages at the meetings responded to his invitation to personally place their trust in Jesus Christ as Savior and Lord.

On Easter Sunday, 1991, I preached on the resurrection of Jesus in the Palace of Congress behind the Kremlin walls. Again, 50 to 80 percent of the 5,000 people present responded to the invitation to receive Christ. The message was carried on nationwide television. According to officials, the broadcast reached a potential audience of 250 million. It is believed that a minimum of 100 million viewed the program and that many millions received Christ as their Savior via television that day.

We have seen a similar response to Jesus of Nazareth around the world.

Perhaps you are wondering, *What's all the excitement? Why do His life and teachings still generate such interest today?*

Jesus is the most remarkable and fascinating person in history. He has inspired more hope, taught more compassion, and shown more love than any other person who has ever lived.

When He walked on earth, Jesus stirred people wherever He went. Crowds followed Him; hands reached out to Him; voices called to Him; people pushed and sometimes trampled one another just to see Him, to hear Him teach, to bring their sick to be healed (Luke 12:1).

Jesus' popularity grew until many wanted to make Him king of the Jews. Once, when He entered Jerusalem, the capital city of Israel, crowds lining the wayside pulled off their cloaks and broke off palm branches to throw in front of Him.

Voices shouted:

"Hosanna to the Son of David!"

"Blessed is he who comes in the name of the Lord!"

"Hosanna in the highest!"

When He entered Jerusalem, the whole city took notice. People gathered asking, "Who is this man?"

Others answered, "This is Jesus, the prophet from Nazareth" (Matthew 21:9–11).

What was there about this Man that caused a stir wherever He went?

History's Greatest Revolutionary

Some time ago, a brilliant, young medical student from another land and a devout follower of an eastern religion came to see me. Through the months I had known him, we had become good friends.

I asked this young man several questions. "Who in your opinion is the greatest leader that the world has ever known? Who has done the most good for mankind?"

After a moment of hesitation, he replied, "I am sure that Jesus has done more good than anyone who has ever lived. I would say that He is the greatest leader."

Then I asked, "Who do you think is the greatest teacher?"

No doubt he considered Socrates, Aristotle, Plato, Confucius, and the other great philosophers of ancient and modern times. But he answered, "The greatest teacher is Jesus."

Finally, I asked, "In your opinion, who in the entire history of man has lived the most holy life?"

Immediately he answered, "There has never been anyone like Jesus."

I have posed these questions to men of all religions, as well as atheists and Communists. The answer from all knowledgeable people is always the same: "Jesus."

Indeed, there has never in history been anyone who could compare with Jesus of Nazareth. He is unique among all the human beings who have ever been born.

Indeed, there has never in history been anyone who could compare with Jesus of Nazareth.

Philip Schaff, well-known historian and author of *The History of the Christian Church*, said:

> *Jesus of Nazareth, without money and arms, conquered more millions than Alexander, Caesar,*

Mohammed, and Napoleon; without science and learning, He shed more light on things human and divine than all the philosophers and scholars combined; without the eloquence of the school, He spoke words of life such as were never spoken before, nor since, and produced effects which lie beyond the reach of orator or poet. Without writing a single line, He has set more pens in motion and furnished themes for more sermons, orations, discussions, works of art, learned volumes, and sweet songs of praise than the whole army of great men of ancient and modern times. Born in a manger and crucified as a malefactor, He now controls the destinies of the civilized world and rules a spiritual empire which embraces one-third of the inhabitants of the globe.[2]

Wherever the true message of Jesus Christ has gone, people and nations have been revolutionized.

Wherever the true message of Jesus Christ has gone, people and nations have been revolutionized, resulting in new life, new hope, and new purpose for living. Indeed, without fear of contradiction, we can regard Jesus Christ as history's greatest revolutionary. Everything about Him was unique: The prophecies of His coming, His birth, His life, His teachings, His miracles, His death, His resurrection, His influence on history and in the lives of hundreds of millions of people.

But many are uncertain about who Jesus was and why He came. Confused about the relevance of His teachings for them today, they question His place in their lives, or wonder, *Who is this Jesus? Why is He different from other men of history? What does He mean to my life today? How can I know Him personally?*

To find answers to these important questions, we will explore several reasons Jesus is considered by knowledgeable people all over the world to be the greatest Man who ever lived:

1. The prophecies of His coming as the Messiah were precise and accurate.

2. The claims He made about Himself were extraordinary and unprecedented.

3. The birth of Jesus was unique.

4. His childhood was unparalleled.

5. His teachings were innovative and life-changing.

6. His death was sacrificial and necessary.

7. His resurrection was history's most revolutionary event.

8. His influence on people and nations through the centuries has changed the world.

Join me now in this exciting adventure to consider the unique life and ministry of Jesus.

NO ORDINARY PERSON

JESUS' CONTEMPORARIES were confused about who He was. At times during His days on earth, even His disciples seemed unsure.

One day, Jesus led them away from the crowds to a deserted area. Imagine the scene. Jesus leaves the disciples to go and pray alone. Someone starts a campfire to warm the dusty-robed men while they wait for their Teacher to return. The crackling sounds of the fire help them to relax after a long, tiring day. They begin to talk about the miracles they have seen the Master perform: the dead raised (Mark 5:42), the demon-possessed delivered (Matthew 9:32,33; 12:22), the sick made well (Matthew 15:30; Luke 8:43,44), the feeding of the five thousand (Matthew 14:19–21).

One of His twelve disciples turns to the others. "I'll never forget the faces of those hungry people! And with only five small loaves and two fish, we fed them all! Wasn't it incredible how the bread and fish kept multiplying?"

Remembering the sight, the other men nod.

The first disciple looks down at his worn hands and continues. "I can't believe there was so much food left!"

"It was a miracle," someone else murmurs.

Another disciple quietly joins in, "I remember how the wind and the waves obeyed Jesus that stormy night on the lake..."

"Jesus Christ alone founded his empire upon love; and, at this hour, millions of men would die for him."

After a time, Jesus rejoins their little group. He lovingly looks at each of them, one by one. With a piercing gaze, He asks them a simple question, "Who do people say I am?" (Mark 8:27).

The disciples pause at the intensity in Jesus' voice. What will they answer?

"Some of them think you are John the Baptist," they reply, "and others say you are Elijah or some other ancient prophet come back to life again" (Mark 8:28, TLB).

Was Jesus just a prophet? A teacher? A good man? Or was He much more than that?

For nearly two thousand years, ordinary people have considered these questions and expressed their views. Great political leaders, religious figures, and scholars have all added their voices to the debate.

No Mere Man

Napoleon Bonaparte declared, "I know men; and I tell you that Jesus Christ is no mere man."[3]

Why would a man who conquered most of Europe and who lived a life of ruthless ambition make such an astonishing statement?

Perhaps Napoleon's own failure made him think about his fate. After his defeat at Waterloo and during his exile on the island of St. Helena, Napoleon had time to reflect on his life and to realize that death awaited even him.

To General Bertrand, a skeptic concerning the deity of Jesus and a faithful officer who had followed him into exile, Napoleon said, "Everything in Christ astonishes me. His spirit overawes me, and His will confounds me...He is truly a being by Himself. His ideas and sentiments, the truth which he announces, His manner of convincing, are not explained either by human organization or by the nature of things.

"Alexander, Caesar, Charlemagne, and myself founded empires. But on what did we rest the creations of our genius? Upon force. Jesus Christ alone founded his empire upon love; and, at this hour, millions of men would die for him."[4]

Many other leaders over the past twenty centuries also have pondered the question, "Who is this Jesus?" Even during Jesus' day, rulers recognized that He was no ordinary person.

Jesus lived and ministered in an unstable political climate. Although Rome generally maintained the peace, political factions and the conditions in Palestine created tensions.

Pontius Pilate, a Roman prelate who held his office for ten years under Emperor Tiberius, was a stubborn, arrogant man who took pains to provoke his Jewish subjects. When he first rode into Jerusalem, he raised Roman banners that he knew would offend the Jews.

Herod Antipas, tetrarch of Galilee and Peraea for about thirty years, and Pilate were enemies. Herod also was unpopular with many of the Jews because he ordered the beheading of John the Baptist (Matthew 14:1–12).

Understandably, the Jewish religious leaders chafed under Roman rule. The Pharisees[5] in particular were looking for the Messiah, a prophesied leader whom they believed would set up a political kingdom and allow the nation of Israel to dominate their oppressors. Consequently, the Pharisees heartily despised anyone who would dare suppress God's people.

Yet when Jesus, the "Man of Peace," came on the scene, these staunch political enemies united to crucify Him.

The jealous religious leaders, feeling threatened by the truth of Jesus' teachings and His integrity, plotted to kill Him. But how could they accomplish the deed? They had no political power to execute anyone.

The chief priests and elders conspired to arrest Jesus by night so that the people wouldn't riot. They bribed Judas, one of Jesus' twelve disciples, to betray Him by leading soldiers to the garden of Gethsemane where Jesus had gone to pray.

The fully armed soldiers marched Jesus to the high priest's house where the religious leaders branded Jesus a blasphemer for claiming to be equal with God and condemned Him to death (Matthew 26:65,66).

His accusers took Him to Pilate. In an effort to compel the Roman governor to carry out their sentence, they falsely charged Jesus with inciting the people to riot and with trying to set up His own kingdom.

Not wanting to deal with the difficult situation, Pilate sent Jesus to Herod. Herod, after ridiculing and mocking Jesus, sent Him back to Pilate. And the religious leaders followed, constantly accusing Him.

The Bible records Pilate's response:

> *"You brought me this man as one who was inciting the people to rebellion. I have examined him in your presence and have found no basis for your charges against Him. Neither has Herod, for he sent him back to us; as you can see, he has done nothing to deserve death"* (Luke 23:14–16).

Attempting to pacify the demands of the accusers, Pilate offered to flog Jesus, then release Him. But the religious leaders wouldn't back down.

"Crucify Him! Crucify Him!" they demanded.

Pilate capitulated. Washing his hands to signify that he wasn't responsible for shedding innocent blood, he turned Jesus over to the executioners.

Ever since Jesus' encounters with Pilate and Herod, the question "Who is this Jesus?" has been the topic of controversy among political leaders. Some have rejected Him and severely persecuted His followers. Many others, however, have shown through what they've said or done that they acknowledged His claims of deity.

Emperor Constantine began his rule as a worshiper of the Persian sun-god Mithra. Tradition tells us that on the eve of a decisive battle, he saw a cross above the sun as it was setting. The cross bore the words, "In this sign conquer." He immediately painted Christian emblems on his soldiers' shields.

The next day Constantine's army defeated its enemies at the Milvian Bridge. As a result, he believed in Christ and became the first Christian emperor in history.

Throughout the years, many rulers followed in the footsteps of Constantine. For example, Clovis, the king of the Franks, converted to Christianity. In A.D. 800, Charlemagne knelt at St. Peter's Church in Rome while the pope placed the imperial crown on his head. And Otto I, king of Germany, came to the rescue of the church, which was battered by warring feudal lords.

In the early 1600s, King James I commissioned the translation of an English Bible.

And Queen Victoria, who reigned over England during most of the 19th century, regularly visited the elderly and poor in the slums of London because of her faith in Jesus.

Most of the Founding Fathers and historic figures of the United States believed deeply in calling upon God to help them rule the affairs of the new nation. Some of them also spoke out about the person of Jesus.

- Patrick Henry, 18th century orator and Revolutionary leader:

   I wish I could leave you my most cherished possession—my faith in Jesus Christ. For with Him you have everything; without Him you have nothing at all.

- Daniel Webster, 19th century orator and influential congressional leader:

   I believe Jesus Christ to be the Son of God. The miracles which he wrought establish in my mind his personal authority, and render it proper for me to believe whatever he asserts...And I believe there is no other way of salvation than through the merits of his atonement.[6]

Modern political leaders have described the change that comes through Christ's work in the heart.

- Dr. Charles Malik, an internationally known statesman, professor of philosophy, and president of the General Assembly of the United Nations in 1959:

  Only those who stay close to Jesus Christ can help others who are far away. Only those who prefer Him to everything else, even to the call of the needy world, can be used of Him for the need of the world... The heart of the whole matter is faith in Jesus Christ.[7]

- James Baker III, U.S. Secretary of State under President George Bush:

  Of course, power brings excitement and invitations to some of the most exclusive gatherings in the world... But power does not bring inner security and fulfillment. That comes only by developing a personal relationship with God, which for me is personified by Jesus Christ. Inner security and real fulfillment comes by faith—not by wielding power in the town where power is king.[8]

Without question, the life and message of Jesus Christ has greatly influenced the course of governments and the destinies of nations. Remove Jesus from the palaces of the world, and the history of the nations would be a completely different story.

Simply a Prophet?

Remember the incident when Jesus asked His disciples, "Who do people say I am?"

The disciples' responses reflected popular belief about Jesus. For example:

- A Samaritan woman at the well was astounded when Jesus knew all about her life. She said, "I can see that you are a prophet" (John 4:19).

- After Jesus raised a widow's son from the dead, onlookers were filled with awe and praised God saying, "A great prophet has appeared among us" (Luke 7:16).

- After hearing Jesus preach, some of the people said, "Surely this man is the Prophet" (John 7:40).

During his lifetime, Jesus gave many startling and accurate prophecies. Here are just a few:

1. He predicted that Judas would betray him (John 6:64,70,71).

2. He foretold His own death and resurrection (Luke 9:22).

3. He predicted the destruction of the temple in Jerusalem (Matthew 24:1,2).

4. He prophesied persecution for His followers in the days ahead (Matthew 10:16–18).

5. Jesus also foresaw world conditions in our present age—such as wars, rumors of wars, earthquakes, and widespread famine (Matthew 24—25).

Who would dare describe these future events in such detail?

Was Jesus simply a prophet? Or was He much more?

The lives and words of past and present religious leaders strongly support their belief in the divinity of Christ.

- Justin Martyr, an early church historian and philosopher who died for his faith in A.D. 166:

  But if you are willing to listen to an account of Him, how we have not been deceived, and shall not cease to confess Him—although men's reproaches be heaped upon us, although the most terrible tyrant compel us to deny Him—I shall prove to you as you stand here that we have not believed empty fables, or words without foundation.[9]

- John F. Walvoord, the late former president of Dallas Theological Seminary:

  The doctrine of the eternity of the Son of God is the most important doctrine of Christology as a whole because if Christ is not eternal then He is a creature who came into existence in time and lacks the quality of eternity and infinity which characterizes God Himself.[10]

- Dr. Walter Martin, the late founder of the Christian Research Institute:

  There is, therefore, only one God by nature, one God who is omnipotent, omniscient, omnipresent, one God who possesses characteristics and attributes that may be imitated but never duplicated in finite creations. When it is said, then, that man is or can be "a god," we must remember that only He, the incarnate Word (Jesus), has the right to the title of deity among men, since He alone is designated "the only begotten God."[11]

Without exception, what men have believed about Jesus of Nazareth—a prophet who was only a man or the God-Man who was the Great Prophet—has set the course of their lives and determined their destiny.

An Educated Guess

Many see Jesus as the greatest teacher in history. No other man has been quoted as often or has inspired as many books and articles. His teachings have given us clear, profound insights into the deepest questions of life.

Though little is recorded of His childhood, what is known of His early years suggests that He had a unique and deep understanding of the heart of God. The Bible records, "Everyone who heard him was amazed at his understanding and his answers" (Luke 2:47).

Those who heard Him speak as an adult were equally stirred. During the three years of His ministry, Jesus traveled throughout what today is the nation of Israel, teaching in the synagogues and healing the sick. Large crowds followed Him everywhere. And Jesus' disciples left everything to walk with and learn from Him.

What kind of teacher could inspire such loyalty?

He was compassionate. Jesus cared about those around Him. God's holy Word says, "When Jesus landed and saw a large crowd, he had compassion on them, because they were like sheep without a shepherd. So he began teaching them many things" (Mark 6:34).

He had a deep love for the hurting and needy. He healed diseases and raised the dead; He visited the sinners and encouraged the outcasts. In fact, His teaching and His compassionate deeds were inseparable.

He was innovative. Jesus used stories and parables to illustrate spiritual truths.

Two of His most well-known parables are "The Good Samaritan" and "The Prodigal Son." He also used familiar items such as sheep, grapevines, farming, and marriage customs to help His listeners understand abstract truths.

He taught through His own example as well.

During His last meal before His crucifixion, He wrapped a towel around His waist and, going from one of His disciples to the other, knelt to wash their feet.

When He finished, He asked, "Do you understand what I have done for you? You call me 'Teacher' and 'Lord,' and rightly so, for that is what I am. Now that I, your Lord and Teacher, have washed your feet, you also should wash one another's feet. I have set you an example that you should do as I have done for you" (John 13:12–15).

He spoke the truth regardless of the consequences. Jesus never changed His message to avoid a scene or to pacify His listeners. In speaking the truth lovingly but bluntly and honestly, He made many enemies—especially among the teachers and religious leaders of Jerusalem.

Because Jesus frequently spoke against the hypocrisy of the scribes and chief priests, they nursed a bitter hatred for Him and eventually succeeded in having Him crucified.

He spoke with revolutionary wisdom and authority. Jesus said things that people had never thought of or spoken before. He declared that His words and wisdom were not His own, but had come directly from His Father, God (John 14:24).

A discourse full of profound truths, His "Sermon on the Mount" reinforces this claim. The Bible records, "When Jesus had finished saying these things, the crowds were amazed at his teaching, because he taught as one who had authority, and not as their teachers of the law" (Matthew 7:28,29).

Without question, the greatest teaching of Jesus was that salvation comes, not by what man does for God, but by what God does for man through His Son (John 3:16–18).

This teaching of salvation by faith in Jesus as God's Messiah, not by works, was unique and revolutionary because ritualistic Judaism and other religions taught that man could reach God or paradise through his good deeds. Jesus repeatedly emphasized good works, but never as the means to salvation (Ephesians 2:8,9).

One day, a group of people approached Jesus and asked, "What must we do to do the works God requires?" Jesus replied, "The work of God is this: to believe in the one he has sent" (John 6:28,29).

His teaching changed lives. Nicodemus was one of the Pharisees, a group of religious leaders who hated Jesus and plotted to destroy Him. When

Nicodemus sought out the Master Teacher late one night, Jesus explained the necessity of spiritual birth to enter the Kingdom of God. His words, "You must be born again" (John 3:7), had a tremendous effect on Nicodemus' life.

Jesus' impact on Nicodemus is clearly evident in subsequent events related to Jesus' arrest and crucifixion. When the chief priests and other Pharisees searched for ways to arrest Jesus, Nicodemus tried to intercede. "Does our law condemn anyone without first hearing him to find out what he is doing?" (John 7:50,51). But his words fell on deaf ears.

Down through the centuries, the lives of hundreds of millions around the world have been changed by His teachings.

Then, after the crucifixion, he accompanied Joseph of Arimathea, a member of the Sanhedrin, to ask Pilate for the body of Jesus. After getting permission to bury the body, Nicodemus took one hundred pounds of spices and helped wrap His remains for a kingly burial (John 19:38–42).

Down through the centuries, the lives of hundreds of millions around the world have been changed by His teachings. Many have reaffirmed the declaration of those who heard him speak, "No man ever spoke like this Man!" (John 7:46, NKJ).

Almost everyone would admit that Jesus of Nazareth was a great teacher. Even His enemies had to acknowledge His timeless wisdom. But was He more than a teacher? Great scholars have expressed their ideas, affirming the person of Christ and His influence on their lives:

- Josephus, Jewish historian of the 1st century:

  About this time there lived Jesus, a wise man, if indeed one ought to call him a man. For he was one who wrought surprising feats and was a teacher of such people as accept the truth gladly.[12]

- Erasmus, 15th and 16th century Dutch scholar, theologian, and writer:

  The sum of all Christian philosophy amounts to this: to place all our hopes in God alone, who by his free grace, without any merit of our own, gives us every thing through Jesus Christ.[13]

- Blaise Pascal, 17th century French mathematician, scientist, and philosopher:

> *Jesus Christ is the center of all, and the goal to which all tends.*[14]

- Feodor Dostoyevsky, 19th century Russian novelist:

> *Even those who have renounced Christianity and attack it, in their inmost being still follow the Christian ideal, for hitherto neither their subtlety nor the ardor of their hearts has been able to create a higher ideal of man and of virtue than the ideal given by Christ of old.*[15]

- Lew Wallace, 19th century lawyer, U.S. General, and author:

> *After six years given to the impartial investigation of Christianity, as to its truth or falsity, I have come to the deliberate conclusion that Jesus Christ was the Messiah of the Jews, the Saviour of the world, and my personal Saviour.*[16]

Some scholars who believed that Jesus was just a man later reversed their thinking out of intellectual honesty and became followers of Jesus.

I was deeply moved while reading about one such scholar in the magazine section of the *Los Angeles Times* early one Sunday morning in about

1949. My eye fell on a picture of a venerable old professor, Dr. Cyril E. M. Joad, and the dramatic story of the change that had taken place in his life.

One of the world's greatest philosophers, Dr. Joad was for years head of the Philosophy Department at the University of London. He and his colleagues—Julian Huxley, Bertrand Russell, H. G. Wells, and George Bernard Shaw—had probably done more to undermine the faith of the collegiate world of the last generation than any other group.

Dr. Joad believed that Jesus was only a man and that God was a part of the universe. Should the universe be destroyed, he taught, God would also be destroyed. He believed that there is no such thing as sin and that man was destined for utopia.

The article described the many years he had been antagonistic toward Christianity and how he denied the existence of sin. However, he said that two world wars and the imminence of another had conclusively demonstrated to him that man was indeed sinful. Now he believed that the only explanation for sin was found in the Bible and that the only solution for sin was the cross of

Jesus Christ. Before his death, Dr. Joad became a zealous follower of Christ. I have in my library one of his last books entitled *The Recovery of Belief*.

Consider too the example of C. S. Lewis. A writer and professor at Oxford and Cambridge Universities in England, he was an agnostic for years. He tried to convince himself that Christianity was invalid. But after a long process of searching for answers, he received Christ as his own Savior and Lord while he was at Oxford. He describes that moment:

> *You must picture me alone in that room in Magdalen, night after night, feeling, whenever my mind lifted for even a second from my work, the steady, unrelenting approach of Him whom I so earnestly desired not to meet. That which I greatly feared had at last come upon me. In the Trinity Term of 1929 I gave in, and admitted that God was God, and knelt and prayed: perhaps, that night, the most dejected and reluctant convert in all England.*[17]

Lewis became a devout follower of Jesus and wrote many books advocating his belief in Christ. In *Mere Christianity*, he writes, "You can shut Him up for a fool, you can spit at Him and kill Him as a demon; or you can fall at His feet and call Him Lord and God. But let us not come up with any patronizing nonsense about His being a great human teacher. He has not left that open to us. He did not intend to."[18] C. S. Lewis concluded that Jesus is indeed more than a good, moral teacher —He is the Savior of the world.

Examine with me the amazing facts concerning the life and ministry of Jesus Christ. Learn what the Old and New Testaments of the Bible have recorded about His nature. Discover the astounding claims He has made about Himself.

This isn't an expedition into dusty, yellowed old books or boring, academic theologies. Rather, it's a thrilling adventure of meeting the One who has changed the world, who has taught the most eminent scholars, who has directed the course of powerful nations and inspired billions of men and women to follow Him. It is a journey into the life and mind of the most revolutionary person in history.

three

PIECES OF THE PUZZLE

THE OLD TESTAMENT, written by many individuals over a period of 1,500 years, records a myriad of astounding predictions. For example, the prophets made detailed forecasts of the rise and fall of nations, the spiritual highs and lows of the nation of Israel, and a future time of terrible calamity and tribulation. Many of these predictions have already been accurately fulfilled. Other events are still in the future.

Not only does the Bible announce what lies ahead, it also sets strict criteria for the prophets who gave the predictions. In the Old Testament, God said to Moses:

> *I will raise up for them a prophet like you from among their brothers; I will put my words in his mouth, and he will tell them everything I command him. If anyone does not listen to my words that the prophet speaks in my name, I myself will call him to account. But a prophet who presumes to speak in my name anything I*

*have not commanded him to say, or a prophet
who speaks in the name of other gods, must be
put to death.*

*You may say to yourselves, "How can we
know when a message has not been spoken by the
LORD?" If what a prophet proclaims in the
name of the LORD does not take place or come
true, that is a message the LORD has not spoken.
That prophet has spoken presumptuously. Do not
be afraid of him (Deuteronomy 18:18–22).*

The most amazing Old Testament prophecies
are those promising a Jewish Messiah. They mys-
tified scholars for thousands of years. Not understanding how to fit the prophecies into a single
picture, the scholars viewed them as pieces of a
giant puzzle. The details seemed to be contradictory or made little sense. Devout Jews, however,
trusted that God would reveal His timely solution.

More than three hundred separate references
to the coming of the Messiah included many
unique details. The Old Testament prophet Micah, for instance, described the precise location of
the Messiah's birth: "But you, Bethlehem Eph-
rathah, though you are little among the thousands
of Judah, yet out of you shall come forth to Me

the One to be ruler in Israel, whose goings forth have been from of old, from everlasting" (Micah 5:2, NKJ).

This small village is the very place where Jesus Christ was born. Is this prophecy a lucky coincidence, or is there certainty that this man Jesus fulfilled every detail predicted of the coming Messiah?

Prophecies of Jesus' Birth

Old Testament Prophecy	Details	Fulfillment in Jesus
Genesis 12:1–3	Descendant of Abraham	Matthew 1:1 Luke 3:34 Matthew 1:2
Genesis 49:10	Descent through the tribe of Judah	Luke 3:33
Micah 5:2	Birth in Bethlehem	Luke 2:4,5,7
Daniel 9:25	Time for His birth	Luke 2:1,2
Isaiah 7:14	Virgin birth	Luke 1:26,31
Isaiah 9:7	Heir to the throne	Luke 1:32,33
Jeremiah 31:15	Slaughter of children	Matthew 2:16–18
Hosea 11:1	Flight to Egypt	Matthew 2:14,15

Space does not allow a complete analysis of prophecies concerning Christ and their fulfillment. But the eight prophecies listed in the chart are typical of the accuracy of all Old Testament predictions.

Now let us apply three standards of accuracy to these prophecies.

No ordinary person has ever selected the time, place, or family into which he was born.

First, *could these predictions have occurred by chance?*

Peter W. Stoner, a professor of mathematics and astronomy, explains the probabilities of eight prophecies being fulfilled in one person. "We find that the chance that any man might have lived down to the present time and fulfilled all eight prophecies is 1 in 10^{17} of being absolute [in mathematical terms, 10^{17} = one hundred quadrillion or 100,000,000,000,000,000]."

To describe how remote a possibility this number represents, Stoner suggests that, after laying one hundred quadrillion silver dollars two feet deep across the state of Texas, we mark one of them and stir the whole mass of them thoroughly. We blindfold one man and ask him to pick up one silver dollar from anywhere in Texas, but he must pick up the marked coin. The probability of his retrieving the exact one is the same likelihood that the prophets had of writing these eight prophecies in their human understanding and of having them all come true, in any one man, from their day to today.

"Now these prophecies were either given by inspiration of God," says Stoner, "or the prophets just wrote them as they thought they should be. In such case the prophets had just one chance in 10^{17} of having them come true in any man, but they all came true in Christ."[19]

And that is not even considering the odds against the other hundreds of prophecies that Jesus fulfilled in detail!

Second, *could Jesus have manipulated events to make it seem as if He fulfilled these predictions?*

No ordinary person has ever selected the time, place, or family into which he was born. Only someone with supernatural power could choose the timing of His birth. How could an ordinary man have engineered the census that brought His parents, Mary and Joseph, to Bethlehem while Jesus was still in His mother's womb? Or have foreseen the flight of His family into Egypt when He was only two years old? Or have fulfilled the many other prophecies of His later life and death?

Third, *could Jesus have guessed the outcome of the seemingly contradictory prophecies of the coming Messiah?*

No historian or any other person could have predicted the manner in which Jesus would come into this world. The fact that the Messiah is connected with two distinct places—Bethlehem and Egypt—and is called *neh-zer*, meaning the "Nazarene," is too conflicting, yet precisely correct, to be simply a guess.[20] The mystery was not solved until Jesus was actually born and fulfilled these prophecies.

Neither could anyone have guessed the precise details concerning His death unless he were more than a man. During the crucifixion, for instance, the soldiers cast lots for His clothing (John 19:24) as King David, one of the most powerful and godly kings of ancient Israel, predicted (Psalm 22:18). We could take other prophecies of the coming Messiah and apply these standards as well. For example:

- The names He would be given (Isaiah 9:6)

- His Galilean ministry (Isaiah 9:1,2)

- His rejection by His own people (Isaiah 53:3)

- His triumphal entry into Jerusalem (Zechariah 9:9)

- His betrayal by a close friend (Psalm 41:9)

- His crucifixion between thieves (Isaiah 53:12)

- His burial with the rich (Isaiah 53:9)

- His resurrection and ascension (Psalm 16:10; 68:18)

Every point of every prophecy concerning Jesus met God's standard for accuracy. No other person in history can claim to have met this requirement. Christ fulfilled 100 percent of all the Old Testament predictions of the birth, life, death, and resurrection of the Messiah!

The New Testament makes an even more revolutionary claim—that Jesus Christ is the center of all biblical prophecy. The Scripture proclaims:

> *God, Who gave to our forefathers many different glimpses of the truth in the words of the prophets, has now, at the end of the present age, given us the Truth in the Son (Hebrews 1:1,2, Phillips).*

And the Book of Ephesians declares:

> *God has allowed us to know the secret of His Plan, and it is this: He purposes in His sovereign will that all human history shall be consummated in Christ, that everything that exists in Heaven or earth shall find its perfection and fulfillment in Him (Ephesians 1:9,10, Phillips).*

The evidence is overwhelming. The precise fulfillment of the immense body of biblical prophecy is found in one unique and revolutionary Man —Jesus of Nazareth. Claiming that He was the predicted One of old, Jesus stepped into time. And the pieces of the prophetic puzzle slipped into place.

So far, we have discovered what political figures, religious leaders, and scholars have said about Jesus. We have also seen how He fulfilled the Old Testament prophecies of the coming Messiah. Now let us look at the claims that Jesus made about Himself.

four

HIS WORDS AND DEEDS

ONE SABBATH the usual crowd gathered in the synagogue at Nazareth. Somber scribes, prestigious religious leaders, and devout laymen patiently waited to hear the Word of God read aloud.

The synagogue attendant brought out a sacred old scroll containing a part of Scripture written hundreds of years before by the prophet Isaiah. Jesus, the carpenter's Son, was chosen to read.

> *The Spirit of the Lord is on me, because he has anointed me to preach good news to the poor. He has sent me to proclaim freedom for the prisoners and recovery of sight for the blind, to release the oppressed, to proclaim the year of the Lord's favor (Luke 4:18,19).*

Then He rolled up the scroll and handed it back to the attendant. Every eye watched as He sat down. Confidently, He looked around and announced, "Today this scripture is fulfilled in your hearing" (Luke 4:21).

What kind of man would dare to announce that He was God's Sent One, the promised Messiah? How could He prove this outrageous claim?

Revolutionary Claims

Jesus of Nazareth made many startling statements about Himself:

He declared He was God: "I and the Father are one...Anyone who has seen me has seen the Father" (John 10:30; 14:9).

Could a man who has accomplished more good for the human race than anyone who has ever lived be deluded about Himself?

He professed to be the only way to God: "I am the way and the truth and the life. No one comes to the Father except through me" (John 14:6).

He affirmed that His words were eternal: "Heaven and earth will pass away, but my words will never pass away" (Mark 13:31).

And He asserted divine authority: "All authority in heaven and on earth has been given to me" (Matthew 28:18).

Consider some the other radical claims He made about Himself.

Jesus Said He Was	Scripture Reference
Able to forgive sins	Mark 2:5–12; Luke 7:48–50; John 8:24
The Son of Man	Matthew 8:20; 11:19; 26:2
The Judge of the world	Matthew 7:21–23
The fulfillment of Scriptures	Matthew 5:17; Luke 24:44
The Bread of life	John 6:35
The Light of the world	John 8:12
The "I Am"	John 8:58; 18:5,6
Divine	Matthew 4:7; 12:6–8; Mark 14:61–64; John 10:30; 17:11
Able to save the lost	Luke 19:10; John 10:9; 11:25,26
Eternal	John 8:58; 17:5
Sinless	John 8:46; 14:30
Able to accomplish God's work	John 17:4

Could a man who has without question accomplished more good for the human race than anyone who has ever lived be deluded about Himself? What man could make these seemingly presumptuous claims unless He truly was God in the flesh? If Jesus is who He claimed to be, how can we know for sure?

Making Sure

Jesus' character and ministry and the witness of those who knew Him best offer abundant evidence to support His radical claims of deity.

The testimony of His character: The Gospels record the life of Jesus. From the beginning, He exhibited gracious and godly qualities unequaled then or since. He demonstrated amazing wisdom, and His understanding and knowledge astounded His followers and dumbfounded His enemies (Matthew 7:28,29; 22:15–46).

His bearing was always under control, and He never failed to please God (Mark 1:10,11). As we have observed, Jesus' compassion was endless— even with the crowds that flocked to touch Him and to be healed (Luke 4:40–43; 8:40–48). He was humble and meek; not even His enemies could accuse Him of pride or pretentiousness. He was patient with all who welcomed Him, did not prefer the rich or famous, and treated children with love and tenderness (Mark 2:14–18; 10:13–16). Jesus spent many hours praying for those who would follow Him and preparing Himself for the suffering that He knew lay ahead on the cross (John 17; Luke 22:40–46). In all ways, His character was pure and selfless.

Jesus was also sinless. When in the desert, He resisted temptation through the power of God's Spirit. Throughout His life and ministry, He was completely obedient and faithful to God. Peter testifies of Jesus, "He committed no sin, and no deceit was found in his mouth" (1 Peter 2:22). The writer of the Book of Hebrews tells us, "We do not have a high priest who is unable to sympathize with our weaknesses, but we have one who has been tempted in every way, just as we are— yet was without sin" (4:15).

Jesus also proved His divine character through His immeasurable love, a passion never equaled in history. Knowing the depths of human depravity, He nevertheless willingly offered Himself as a sacrifice to pay for every sin and evil committed by the rebellious human beings He had created. He endured the wrath of His Father toward sin in order to heal and restore each person who would accept His free gift of everlasting life (Romans 5:1,2; 5:8–10). Only God in the flesh could so unselfishly love such unlovely creatures!

The proof of His ministry: Jesus proclaimed that He was indeed the Son of God. Consider these proofs:

1. He fulfilled Old Testament Scriptures concerning His birth, life, death, and resurrection (Isaiah 7:14; 9:1,2; 53:3–12; Psalm 22:16–18; 16:10; Zechariah 9:9).

2. The wisdom of His teachings and His authoritative understanding of God's holy Word astounded all who heard Him (Matthew 7:28, 29; 22:15,16; John 6:68).

3. He worked miracles of healing, cast out demons, commanded the seas and weather, and performed other extraordinary acts (Mark 1:34, 39–42; 4:37–41; John 11:39–44).

4. He quietly and matter-of-factly received worship and devotion from His followers and from the crowds (Matthew 14:33; John 9:38; 12:13).

5. He publicly pardoned sin (Mark 2:5–12).

6. He predicted future events, including His own death and resurrection and the destruction of the temple at Jerusalem (Matthew 23:37—24:2; Mark 8:31).

7. He gave power to His followers and sent them out to cast out demons and heal the sick (Matthew 10:1).

8. He perfectly obeyed God's commands, even to the point of crucifixion (Luke 22:42; 23:44–48; Phil. 2:8).

9. He displayed divine power through His resurrection and ascension (John 20; Acts 1:1–11).

Every miracle Jesus performed, every sermon He preached, every lesson He taught further proved that He was who He claimed to be—the Son of God, equal with God the Father.

The witness of His followers: Jesus drew many responses from people who heard His claims. Some worshiped Him as did the crowd during His triumphal entry into Jerusalem. A leper whom Jesus healed fell at His feet (Matthew 8:2). So did the man who was born blind (John 9:35–39). His disciples worshiped Him (Matthew 14:33). Many people who saw Him day after day were convinced that He was more than a man (John 11:23–25).

The events following His death also prove that Jesus was the Messiah. Before His death, for example, the disciples were timid, frightened men. They deserted Him when He was arrested, cowered during His trial, and stood at a distance when He was crucified.

Yet later, these same men, convinced of His resurrection and filled with the Holy Spirit, revolutionized the world with His teachings. They and other believers endured hardship and persecution, and many were martyred for their Savior and Lord.

The testimonies of some of His closest followers are recorded in the New Testament. Peter begins one of his epistles, "Simon Peter, a servant and apostle of Jesus Christ, to those who through the righteousness of our *God and Savior Jesus Christ* have received a faith as precious as ours" (2 Peter 1:1). John, the beloved disciple of Jesus, says of Him, "No one has seen God at any time. The only begotten Son, who is in the bosom of the Father, He has declared Him" (John 1:18, NKJ).

These Christians proved through their transformed lives that Jesus Christ is truly the only One who can change the human heart.

Stephen, the first martyr for Christ, called upon his Savior as he was being stoned, "*Lord Jesus*, receive my spirit" (Acts 7:59). And Paul writes, "We wait for the blessed hope—the glorious appearing of our *great God and Savior, Jesus Christ*" (Titus 2:13). These and many other New Testament Christians proved through their transformed lives that Jesus Christ is truly the only One who can change the human heart.

Through the centuries, hundreds of millions have found the reality of Jesus' claims to be true in their lives.

For almost sixty years, it has been my personal privilege to have worked with and introduced many thousands of students, professors, and other adults in all walks of life to Jesus Christ. Thousands have shared with me their profound gratitude for the way Jesus has changed their lives and expressed their eternal thanks for all that He has done and is doing for them. Certainly, this is one of the greatest proofs that Jesus is everything He claimed to be.

But before we can completely answer the question, "Who is this Jesus?", we must also examine His mission and how He fulfilled it.

five

ONE OF A KIND

MAN HAS LONG searched for the Creator of life and the answers to age-old questions: Who am I? Why am I here? Where did I come from? Where am I going?

Just imagine it—the moment of man's creation. From the ground God scoops fresh earth, molding it carefully into a marvelous new form. The body lies before its Sculptor ready for life. With a smile of satisfaction, the Maker bends low and breathes deeply into the still figure. The breath of life fills the lungs.

A wave of warmth surges through the body, infusing it with strength.

The figure speaks slowly, "Who am I?"

His Maker smiles. "You are man, and your name is Adam. I have made you this day as the crown of My creatures."

"Why am I here?" Adam rises to his feet.

"To fellowship with Me and bring glory to My name!" the Holy One replies.

"What is my future?"

"I will create from your rib a companion, and you shall be man and wife. Your destiny is to multiply yourselves, fill the earth with your kind, and have dominion over all that I have made."

The Sculptor peers admiringly at His creation. The pleasure of God echoes throughout the heavens in triumph, "It is very good" (adapted from Genesis 1 and 2). So began the journey of man.

Destiny Turns to Disaster

God created man with a free will—the ability to choose his own destiny—and put within him the principle and power of obedience. With the knowledge of God's will, Adam knew the rewards of obedience and the penalty for disobedience. But would he obey?

As a test, God placed a tree in the Garden of Eden. Eating of its fruit would destroy Adam's innocence and enable him to know good and evil, which would result in his death and the fall of the human race. "You must not eat from the tree of the knowledge of good and evil," God warned, "for when you eat of it you will surely die" (Genesis 2:17).

64

It's a familiar story—how the serpent, Satan,[21] beguiled Eve, who ate of the forbidden fruit and then gave it to her husband. Adam knew the consequences of his act but chose to eat the fruit anyway. His act of disobedience caused "the Fall" of mankind from innocence and separated humanity from the loving Creator (Genesis 3).

The consequences were devastating.

The Fall sabotaged God's plan for man by usurping the authority that belongs to God and violating man's dependence upon Him. As man became independent of his Creator, his eternal tie with God was broken.

Pain, hardship, and sorrow came. The woman suffered in childbearing. For the man, the ground was cursed and no longer yielded good fruit without cultivation. Thorns and thistles overran the land. As a result, exhausting physical labor became his lot. Driven from the Garden of God, humanity faced an unknown future in a cursed and desolate world (Genesis 3:16–19,22–24).

Death—separation from God—condemned man to eternal, spiritual darkness and consigned him to Satan's kingdom. In the process, fear of God replaced fellowship with God, and shame over sin obscured the joy of innocence (Genesis 3:1–19; Romans 5:12; John 3:19).

Mankind in this moment of self-will lost the seed of eternal life. Now, instead of living forever, his days were numbered, his destiny ruined. The writer of the Old Testament Book of Ecclesiastes poignantly describes this disaster.

> *This only have I found: God made mankind upright, but men have gone in search of many schemes . . . This is the evil in everything that happens under the sun: The same destiny overtakes all. The hearts of men, moreover, are full of evil and there is madness in their hearts while they live, and afterward they join the dead (Ecclesiastes 7:29; 9:3).*

In their disobedience, Adam and Eve followed a crafty old pied piper, Satan, into a tunnel of disbelief and deceit. Emerging from the other end, they and all humanity after them had to face the tragic result of their waywardness. They could no longer view their destiny clearly. The results of their defiance are visible everywhere—dysfunction, disease, decay, and death.

The question is often asked, "Why should billions of people suffer because of the sin and disobedience of one man, Adam?" Because he was the representative of mankind down through the ages. Let me explain.

In modern history, we have seen the rise of many ruthless dictators such as Adolph Hitler, Joseph Stalin, the Ayatollah Khomeini, and Saddam Hussein. The decisions these men made affected the lives of every citizen of their countries. The deeds of these ungodly leaders caused injury and death to many millions of men, women, and children.

Similarly, Adam's sin produced death and decay for those he represents. Every man and woman born on this earth has suffered for Adam's willful disobedience. Thus the writer of Ecclesiastes observes, "Death is the destiny of every man; the living should take this to heart" (Ecclesiastes 7:2).

He Came for You

The transgression of Adam and Eve was a voluntary elevation of the will of man over the will of God. It was a deliberate trespass of a divinely marked boundary, a decision to exchange the word of the living God for the lie of His depraved enemy. Each human being born since Adam has inherited this tendency to go his own way. It is called the sin nature.

Man's self-will is characterized by an attitude of active rebellion or passive indifference. Because of sin, he is by nature degenerate and corrupt. With his understanding darkened and conscience defiled, his thoughts and affections are worldly, sensual, and "full of evil."

In this condition, man is destitute of God's love, undeserving of His forgiveness, filled with hostility to all that is godly, possessed of a nature that is constantly on the downgrade, and in bondage to a dominion from which he cannot free himself (John 5:42; Romans 8:7; 7:18,23,24).

With man in such a state, how could he ever be reunited with his Creator? How could he be restored to fellowship and fulfill his intended destiny? Man needed to be redeemed. But who could be his redeemer?

God had a wonderful plan. Not an afterthought of the Fall, it was a glorious preplanned work that He conceived before the creation of man (Ephesians 1:3–14). The plan involved God's unconditional love and perfect justice.

Imagine getting a traffic ticket for speeding. When you show up in court, your own father is the judge. Would it be fair for him to fine everyone else who has a ticket, but excuse you because you are his child? Of course not.

Suppose, then, he fines you one hundred dollars. Since you do not have the money, you must spend thirty days in jail. But because he loves you, your father steps down from the judge's bench and pays the fine for you. Justice is satisfied; you go free. The only condition is that you accept your father's payment.

Coming to this world and taking man's place, Jesus accepted the full penalty for man's sin.

Similarly, man could not redeem himself. The substitute had to be a man to take the place of man. He had to be sinless to die for the sinner. Since humanity could not provide such a Redeemer, that Savior had to come from God.

To this purpose, God in the person of His only begotten Son, Jesus Christ, conceived by the Holy Spirit and born of a virgin, offered Himself as the required substitute. Coming to this world and taking man's place, He accepted the full penalty for man's sin (John 3:16–18; Isaiah 53:5,6; 1 Corinthians 15:3,4; 2 Corinthians 5:21; 1 Peter 2:24; 3:18; Romans 5:6–8). Because He was man, He could die, and because He was God, He could die for the sins of the whole world.

Jesus Came With a Sense of Mission

Jesus said to Zacchaeus, the corrupt tax collector, "Today salvation has come to this house...For the Son of Man came to seek and to save what was lost" (Luke 19:9,10). One cannot read the New Testament accounts of the life of Christ without realizing that this was His mission.

One cannot read the New Testament accounts of the life of Christ without realizing that this was His mission.

From His earliest youth and throughout His life, Jesus knew He was a man of destiny. The Bible shows us how clearly He understood His mission and purpose.

First, *as a boy of twelve, He claimed to be doing God's will.* He had come with his parents to Jerusalem to celebrate the Feast of the Passover, a Jewish holy festival. When they left for home, He lingered behind and was not missed by them until the next day. Joseph and Mary found Him three days later sitting among the scholars, "discussing deep questions with them and amazing everyone with his understanding and answers" (Luke 2:46, TLB).

When asked why He had stayed behind, Jesus was surprised—as though His parents should have known. "Why is it that you sought Me? Did you not know that I must be about My Father's business?" (Luke 2:49, NKJ).

Second, *God proclaimed Jesus His beloved Son.* When Jesus was baptized by the prophet John the Baptist in the Jordan River, the heavens opened to Him, "and he saw the Spirit of God descending like a dove and lighting on him. And a voice from heaven said, 'This is my Son, whom I love; with him I am well pleased'" (Matthew 3:16,17).

Third, *Jesus' selection of His disciples demonstrated an awareness of His Messianic mission.* When He called Nathanael to be His disciple, Jesus said, "You will even see heaven open and the angels of God coming back and forth to me, the Messiah" (John 1:51, TLB).

Fourth, *Jesus acknowledged His eternal glory.* He prayed, "Father, the time has come...I have brought you glory on earth by completing the work you gave me to do. And now, Father, glorify me in your presence with the glory I had with you before the world began" (John 17:1,4,5). Here we see Jesus approaching His finest hour with the knowledge of His eternal existence and destiny.

How He Fulfilled His Mission

With such a great task before Him, how did Christ carry out His mission? The story begins with a young virgin in Nazareth. The New Testament records this startling event:

> *God sent the angel Gabriel to Nazareth, a village in Galilee, to a virgin, Mary, engaged to be married to a man named Joseph...*
>
> *Gabriel appeared to her and said, "Congratulations, favored lady! The Lord is with you!"*
>
> *Confused and disturbed, Mary tried to think what the angel could mean.*
>
> *"Don't be frightened, Mary," the angel told her, "for God has decided to wonderfully bless you! Very soon now, you will become pregnant and have a baby boy, and you are to name him 'Jesus.' He shall be very great and shall be called the Son of God..."*
>
> *Mary asked the angel, "But how can I have a baby? I am a virgin."*
>
> *The angel replied, "The Holy Spirit shall*

72

*come upon you, and the power of God shall over-
shadow you; so the baby born to you will be ut-
terly holy—the Son of God...*"

*Mary said, "I am the Lord's servant, and I
am willing to do whatever he wants. May everything you said come true." And then the angel
disappeared (Luke 1:26–38, TLB).*

As Herbert Lockyer explains, Christ's virgin
birth simply means that, "contrary to the course
of nature, Jesus was divinely conceived by the
Holy Spirit in the womb of Mary. In such a con-
ception, deity and humanity were fused together
and Jesus came forth as the God-Man."[22] The
whole superstructure of the Christian faith de-
pends upon this fact.

Had Jesus been born of a mortal man as well
as a mortal woman, He would not have been sinless nor the only Son of God as He claimed, but a
mere man with no power to forgive sin. In turn,
we would have been deprived of His unique character, and we would have been separated from
God, lost in our sins forever, and denied our eternal destiny.

Because of His virgin birth, Jesus has a dual
nature: He is both the Son of God and the Son of

Man. Our finite minds cannot begin to comprehend what that means, but it is true. In this personal union of the human and divine natures in Christ, the eternal Son of God took upon Himself a complete, but sinless, human nature and became Man (Philippians 2:6–8; John 1:1–4,14; Romans 1:2–5; 1 Timothy 3:16; Hebrews 2:14). As the Son of God, His mission was to go to the cross and pay the penalty for our sins, which no human being could accomplish. As the Son of Man, His purpose was to identify with all aspects of our humanity. And because of His unique nature, Jesus could do so without sin (Hebrews 4:15).

Christ's dual nature is vital to God's plan of deliverance. Finis Jennings Dake in his commentary, *God's Plan for Man*, writes:

> *It was not only important that He have two natures, human and divine, for the sake of man, but also for the sake of God, to be a true mediator between God and man...As God He can uphold the dignity of Deity, and as man He can be truly sympathetic and meet the needs of man.*[23]

Jesus alone is able to bridge the gulf between the holiness of God and the sinfulness of man.

Only through Him do we find the way to God and experience His love and forgiveness and the assurance of eternal life.

Our Lord is unique not only in His revolutionary birth and nature, but in how He lived and in what He taught as well. As the Son of Man, Jesus is the ideal of what God wants us to become.

In His absolute submission to God the Father, in His full surrender to God's Holy Spirit, in His unquestioning obedience to the will of God, in His total triumph over temptation, in His sinless life and miraculous ministry, in His purposeful prayers, Jesus is our supreme example.

At the heart of these marvelous qualities is Christ's matchless and infinite love. Unlike the Hollywood image of love, which is based on lust and selfishness, Christ's love is selfless, unconditional, and sacrificial. This sacrificial love cost Jesus His life.

With two thousand years of advances in education, technology, philosophy, and science, we have never produced another who is worthy to be compared with Jesus. His divinity and humanity are without parallel among men.

But the ultimate expression of His revolutionary life was His death. Jesus Christ was the only man in all of history who was born to die. His death had a fourfold purpose:

1. To pay the penalty of our sin and rescue us from the sentence of death.

2. To provide the basis on which God could set forth His righteousness and yet pardon sinful man.

3. To liberate us from Satan's kingdom.

4. To reconcile all who would repent of their sins to God.

Paul brings this purpose into focus in one of his letters:

> *It was through what his Son did that God cleared a path for everything to come to him— all things in heaven and on earth—for Christ's death on the cross has made peace with God for all by his blood . . . and now as a result Christ has brought you into the very presence of God, and you are standing there before him with nothing left against you . . . ; the only condition is that you fully believe the Truth, standing in it steadfast and firm, strong in the Lord, convinced of the Good News that Jesus died for you, and nev-*

er shifting from trusting him to save you (Colossians 1:20–23, TLB).

Hundreds of millions of people around the world have discovered this marvelous path. The Bible records that God has liberated us "out of the darkness and gloom of Satan's kingdom and brought us into the Kingdom of his dear Son, who bought our freedom with his blood and forgave us all our sins" (Colossians 1:13,14, TLB). If you have trusted Jesus Christ as your Savior and Lord, you too are a living testimony of this truth.

Jesus' death was only part of the redemptive process. Without His resurrection and ascension, His sacrifice would have been incomplete, and we would have remained under the penalty of death. The resurrection, as we shall see, is the final proof that Jesus Christ is who He claimed to be. And His ascension into heaven signified the completion of His mission on earth as the Savior who made possible man's restoration to his original destiny.

six

REVOLUTIONARY RESURRECTION

THE VALIDITY OF Jesus' claims about Himself rests on whether He rose from the dead or stayed in the grave.

During my ministry, which began in 1945, I have met many skeptics of the resurrection, both students and laymen alike. Some have said that to believe in a risen Christ is nothing more than a blind leap of faith with little or no basis in truth. When confronted with the facts, however, those who were intellectually honest have been forced to admit that the resurrection is a historical event based on irrefutable proofs.

On my spiritual journey from agnosticism to a vital, living faith in Christ, I too had a problem with the resurrection. How could a human being who had died be raised from the dead? I was willing to believe, but not at the risk of losing my intellectual integrity. So I began to investigate the evidence.

Evidences of the Resurrection

The following evidence brought me to a firm conviction that a bodily resurrection is the only explanation for Christ's empty tomb.

Christ predicted His resurrection. The Bible records, "From that time on Jesus began to explain to his disciples that he must go to Jerusalem and suffer many things…and that he must be killed and on the third day be raised to life" (Matthew 16:21). Even though His followers did not understand what He was telling them at the time, they remembered His words and recorded them. Matthew, Mark, and Luke each describe the predictions in their accounts of Christ's life.

Jesus made numerous appearances to His followers. On at least ten occasions after His death, Jesus appeared to those who had known Him. In each instance, He related to them as the living, loving Savior. He comforted the mourners outside His tomb on Sunday morning (Matthew 28:1–10). On the road to Emmaus, He explained things about Himself from the Old Testament (Luke 24:13–32). Later, He ate in their presence and invited them to touch Him. Scripture records that Jesus was seen by more than five hundred at one time (1 Corinthians 15:3–6). Each time, His friends were assured that He was alive and in bodily form.

A few people could have agreed to a deception, but how can one explain the collaboration of five hundred people? History convinces me that these witnesses actually saw Jesus with their own eyes following His resurrection.

The unrelenting faith of the disciples convinces me of the resurrection. Those disciples who were once so afraid that they deserted their Lord now courageously proclaimed this news, risking their lives to preach the facts of the resurrection of Jesus. Most of them died as martyrs proclaiming Jesus' death and resurrection. Their bold and courageous behavior does not make sense unless they knew with absolute certainty that Jesus had been raised from the dead.

The growth of the Christian church confirms the resurrection. Peter's first sermon, which dealt with Christ's resurrection, stirred people to receive Him as their living Savior. Luke records the thrilling results: "Those who accepted his message were baptized, and about three thousand were added to their number that day" (Acts 2:41). And that group of believers has multiplied until now it reaches around the world. Today, there are hundreds of millions of believers—more than ever in history. Surely, without a powerful, resurrected, living Founder, the Christian church would never have been born or would have slowly faded and eventually died.

The testimony of hundreds of millions of transformed lives through the centuries shows the power of the resurrection. Second Corinthians 5:17 gives glorious assurance that everyone who truly receives Jesus Christ into their lives will be forever changed. Countless numbers who have accepted Jesus Christ as their Savior and Lord give evidence of His resurrection power to break the bonds of sin and produce righteousness and peace in their lives. Many have been delivered from addictions. The destitute and despairing have found hope. Broken marriages have been restored. Sufferers have been comforted. The most conclusive proof for the resurrection of Jesus Christ is that He is living within believers today in all of His resurrected life and transforming power.

Indeed, the resurrection sets Christianity apart from all the religions of the world. No religion can claim that its founder was raised from the dead and that he lives today in the hearts of his followers. No other religious leader has broken the power of death and conquered sin. Only Christianity is based on the historical evidence of a risen Christ and an empty tomb.

Significance of the Resurrection

The resurrection confirms that Jesus is who He claimed to be. Let us consider the magnitude of this event.

The resurrection proved that Christ was divine. The fact that Jesus Christ died on the cross in itself does not prove He is God. Many have died on a cross. Jesus proved His deity by fulfilling the prophecies of His death and by returning from the grave. The Bible declares that "by being raised from the dead [Christ] was proved to be the mighty Son of God, with the holy nature of God himself" (Romans 1:4, TLB).

The resurrection proved Christ's power to forgive sin. If Jesus had not been raised from the dead, His claim to be the Savior of mankind would be empty. His death would be reduced to that of an ordinary man.

The Bible asserts, "If Christ has not been raised, your faith is futile; you are still in your sins" (1 Corinthians 15:17). But by rising from the dead, Jesus proved His authority and power to break the bonds of sin and to assure forgiveness and eternal life to all who accept His gift of salvation.

The resurrection revealed Christ's power over death. The Bible records, "Christ rose from the dead and will never die again. Death no longer has any power over him" (Romans 6:9, TLB). The resurrection secured our victory over death as well and "lifted us up from the grave into glory along with Christ, where we sit with him in the heavenly realms" (Ephesians 2:6, TLB).

The resurrection defeated God's enemy. One cannot begin to fathom the depth of enmity between Satan and God. From the moment of his original rebellion until the day of the cross, the devil fought viciously and cunningly to overthrow the kingdom of God. He spoiled God's greatest creation in the Garden of Eden, and having ruined man, he struggled fiendishly to thwart the coming of the Savior who would restore mankind to its original destiny.

Satan must have thought that he had dealt the final and decisive blow in this age-old war when Jesus went to the cross. By killing the Son of God, he had ruined God's plan for redemption. But this was the devil's most serious miscalculation. The cross was *heaven's* triumph. And when

Jesus Christ arose, the power of sin and death was forever shattered.

Christ's conquest is also the believer's victory. Because of the resurrection, Christians need never fear Satan or death again.

Completing His Mission

As He faced His own death, Jesus began preparing His followers to carry on His work. He emphasized the two most important commandments. The first is to "'Love the Lord your God with all your heart and with all your soul and with all your mind and with all your strength.' The second is this: 'Love your neighbor as yourself'" (Mark 12:30,31).

For forty days after His death and resurrection, Christ appeared many times to His followers. On one occasion, He gathered His remaining eleven disciples on a mountain in Galilee and gave them His "Great Commission." He said, "Go and make disciples of all nations, baptizing them in the name of the Father and of the Son and of the Holy Spirit, and teaching them to obey everything I have commanded you. And surely I am with you always" (Matthew 28:19,20). His instructions were a revolutionary strategy for fulfilling the two commandments He had given by proclaiming the Good News of God's love and forgiveness to the world. Later, on the Mount of Olives, He admonished His disciples to wait in Jerusalem until they were filled with the Holy Spirit and then to take His message to Jerusalem, Judea, Samaria, and to the ends of the world (Acts 1:8).

Immediately after, He rose skyward and disappeared into the clouds, leaving the disciples staring after Him in amazed wonder.

The ascension of Christ was the final act in the drama of redemption. His mission completed, Jesus Christ was exalted to His former glory. The Gospel of John records the prayer Jesus prayed just before He died:

> *Father, the time has come. Glorify your Son, that your Son may glorify you. For you granted him authority over all people that he might give eternal life to all those you have given him. Now this is eternal life: that they may know you, the only true God, and Jesus Christ, whom you have sent. I have brought you glory on earth by completing the work you gave me to do. And now, Father, glorify me in your presence with the glory I had with you before the world began (John 17:1–5).*

From His glorified position in heaven, Jesus now intercedes before God on our behalf as our High Priest. Formerly, a high priest offered sacrifices for the sins of the people. In completing the redemptive process, Jesus took upon Himself this high priestly role. The New Testament explains, "Because Jesus lives forever, he has a permanent priesthood. Therefore he is able to save completely those who come to God through him, because he always lives to intercede for them" (Hebrews 7:24,25).

The resurrection of Jesus Christ ranks as history's most revolutionary event. One cannot deny that He shook the world in His day. But His life just as dramatically has shaped the course of history to our time.

seven

HE CHANGED THE WORLD

NO OTHER PERSON in history has influenced the world for good more than Jesus Christ. His life and message have greatly changed the lives of people and nations. History is His Story. Remove Jesus of Nazareth from history, and it would be a completely different story.

For the past 2,000 years, He has been the centerpiece of humanity. Charles Spurgeon, an English theologian, wrote:

> *Christ is the great central fact in the world's history. To him everything looks forward or backward. All the lines of history converge upon him. All the great purposes of God culminate in him. The greatest and most momentous fact which the history of the world records is the fact of his birth.*[24]

Consider today's date on your calendar. It gives witness to the fact that Jesus of Nazareth, the Christ, lived on the earth. B.C. means "before

Christ"; A.D., *anno Domini*, is the Latin phrase translated "in the year of our Lord."

Believers who spread Christianity demonstrated an active, transforming energy and pure integrity that affected every society they touched. Samuel Zwemer, a professor of missions at Princeton Theological Seminary in the early 1900s, said:

> *The gospel not only converts the individual, but it changes society. On every mission field, from the days of William Carey, the missionaries carried a real, social gospel. They established standards of hygiene and purity, promoted industry, elevated womanhood, restrained anti-social customs, abolished cannibalism, human sacrifice and cruelty, organized famine relief, checked tribal wars, and changed the social structure of society.*

It would be impossible to show the magnitude of Christ's influence on the world.

It would be impossible to show the magnitude of Christ's influence on the world. I can only help you step closer to the mural of history to examine a few of the ways in which His life and message have made a dramatic difference in civilization.

Social Reform

Jesus fed the hungry, healed the sick, comforted the bereaved, and loved the outcast.

Believers through the centuries have followed His example. The more serious the social problems, the greater the desire of Christian men and women to find remedies for these ills.

From the beginning, the followers of Jesus treated individuals with a dignity and worth unknown to their pagan culture. As a result, wherever missionaries took the true gospel of Christ, social conditions dramatically improved and cultures were enriched.

Early Christians, for example, helped soften the harshness of Roman slavery and contributed to its decline. They taught reverence for womanhood, which was unknown in Roman society, and stressed the permanence and sacredness of marriage.

The Reformation stirred believers toward one of the greatest movements of social reform in history. Among other changes, Christians moved for prison reform and built orphanages.

In the 19th century, religious revivals stirred devout men and women to push for new social reforms. Efforts included the formation of groups to combat alcohol abuse, to fight for the abolition of slavery, and to give women the right to vote. It was the clergy who set up the first agencies to provide social services.

Zealous missionaries established orphanages, provided famine relief, raised the status of women, and worked to abolish cruel social customs, including cannibalism and human sacrifice. Other Christian leaders, such as William Booth, who founded the Salvation Army, began endeavors to relieve human suffering in urban areas.

Today, committed Christians are fighting to eliminate abortion and halt euthanasia; they are working diligently to reduce child abuse, drug addiction, and alcoholism; they are seeking to eliminate pornography. Christian organizations are coordinating actions against age-old problems such as prejudice, poverty, famine, and family dysfunction.

Medicine

Jesus Christ also felt concern for those who suffered from disease and handicaps. He cured the leper, healed the lame, and gave sight to the blind. In the process, He taught His disciples to show the same compassion.

Believers have cared for the sick ever since the time of Christ. By the Medieval period, the church was establishing hospices and hospitals. And during the 18th and 19th centuries, hospitals became centers for medical training and research as well as for healing. New institutions, such as the Red Cross, were mostly the work of individual believers and Christian denominations or churches. These organizations arose to care for the mentally ill, encourage public health education, and relieve human suffering.

Although much of Western society, inspired by Christian example, now provides health care through secular sources, the medical work of missions continues in many parts of the world. For multitudes of disadvantaged people, medical supplies, immunizations, and surgical and hospice care come from missionaries and native Christians who bring the love of Christ in word and deed.

Business

The principles Jesus taught have made an impact on the world of business. The early church taught the dignity of labor, and believers were admonished to work hard and to shun laziness. During the Middle Ages, monasteries improved agriculture by developing crop yield and methods of tillage. The church also insisted on a just price for goods and fair wages for the worker.

The Reformation inspired dramatic changes in the world of business. By emphasizing every vocation as a "call" from God, Christians encouraged the growth of a new urban middle class. This new spirit of commerce stimulated navigational exploration and the settlement of unknown lands.

The turbulence of industrialization, urbanization, and immigration in the 18th and 19th centuries brought hardship and poverty to millions of people across Europe and North America. Under the leadership of John Wesley and George Whitefield, many Christians, individually and in groups, began striving for reform in the workplace. Some fought for regulations to protect women and children in mines and industry. Others opposed forced labor, helped enact child labor laws, and formed labor unions.

In the 20th century, many godly men such as J. L. Kraft of Kraft Cheese and J. C. Penney, who founded a merchandizing empire by that name, built businesses based on biblical principles. They funneled large percentages of their profits into the church or worthy social projects. They sought to make work conditions fair and profitable for their employees and gave of their personal wealth and time to spread the gospel of Christ.

Science

Christianity has had a profound influence upon science as well. The biblical view of an orderly and dependable universe formed and held together by a divine Creator became the foundation for many of history's scientific discoveries. Christ's teaching inspired the thinking of many celebrated forerunners of modern science, including Roger Bacon, Nicolaus Copernicus, Johannes Kepler, Galileo, Blaise Pascal, and Isaac Newton. Christian thought also was foundational to applied science—fostering industrialization, medical progress, space research, and advances in other scientific fields.

During the 19th and 20th centuries, however, many scientists have tried to separate science and religion, falsely asserting that natural processes prove God does not exist. Unable to prove or disprove the existence of God, they conveniently overlook the evidential order of the universe that early scientists looked for because of their belief in God.

But recent discoveries and developments show the emptiness of science without Christ. The problems of ecological imbalances stemming from scientific progress, the waste of resources, the ability to tamper with human genes, the ethics of test-tube fertilization, and of nuclear and chemical weapons, point to the possible abuses of science divorced from God's design and standards. Today, an increasing number of scientists are joining a long list of famous forerunners who embraced a biblical faith in Christ.

Law and Government

Christian principles have had a significant effect on law and government. The early Christians promoted justice. Converted politicians worked for legislation on behalf of widows, orphans, and the poor, and against immoral and harsh practices. Christ's influence strengthened resistance to barbaric invasions and brought orderly living to pagan tribes.

English common law was developed from the idea that man is accountable to a higher law based on the Bible. Similarly, biblical principles of freedom and justice provided a basis for the Constitution of the United States.

Christianity influenced many great statesmen. The first President of the United States, George Washington, began and ended each day on his knees in prayer and often quoted the Bible in his speeches and writings. President Abraham Lincoln regularly sought the counsel of God in making major decisions.

In the mid 1950s, President Dwight D. Eisenhower helped give significance to the newly established National Day of Prayer for Americans.[25] He believed he was called by God to give leadership to spiritual renewal in the United States.

Biblical principles of freedom and justice provided a basis for the Constitution of the United States.

In many countries, especially much of the continent of Africa, mission schools educated a large proportion of the national leadership. Jomo Kenyatta, the first president of Kenya, attended school at the Church of Scotland mission in Kikuyu. He served three terms. Much of Kenya's post-independence political stability can be attributed to Kenyatta's wise leadership.

In Zambia, Kenneth David Kaunda received his early training at the Lubwe Mission School. He later became a missionary for the Livingstone

Mission, a spokesman for black Africans, and the president of his country. His Christian beliefs influenced his ideology for the development of Zambia. He was also considered by many as one of Africa's most honorable statesmen.

Arts and Culture

Christian ideals are reflected in art and culture. The early Christians redirected the pagan focus of the arts where they lived. Beginning with the New Testament, believers created a vast new literature in a dying Roman civilization. By the 6th century, the arts were preserved and developed almost exclusively within the church.

During the Medieval period, culture revolved around the cathedral. Mosaics, sculptures, paintings, stained glass, even new forms of architecture were displayed in the house of God. Music, drama, art, and much of literature centered around Christian themes.

As the Protestant movement expanded and enhanced the message of the church, artists were inspired by many different Christian schools of thought. DaVinci, Michelangelo, and Raphael expressed their art and sculpture with epic biblical themes. The dynamic spiritual music of Bach,

Beethoven, and Handel rings down through the ages. John Bunyan, Dante, and Milton centered their literature around scriptural motifs. Even artists who claimed no allegiance to Jesus Christ used Christian symbols and imagery in their work.

Education

One of the most consistent and important influences of Jesus Christ lies in education. In the first centuries, the church took upon itself the task of increasing literacy so that every believer could read the words of Jesus.

During the Dark Ages, the church alone maintained schools, founded universities that became seats of intellectual activity, and developed great libraries. Eventually the Reformation brought learning to the masses, and literacy spread among women. A reconstruction of educational methods and curriculum resulted. Hundreds of Christian colleges were established—many of which are listed today among the most prestigious institutions in the world.

Wherever Christian missionaries settled, a rise in literacy followed. These devout believers gave written form to hundreds of languages and taught millions of people to read and write. Today, many mission groups continue their work in disadvantaged areas of the world.

The influence of Jesus is still revolutionizing our world. Christianity has spanned cultural diversities, prejudice barriers, and political differences.

Truly, Jesus Christ is the only answer to our world's needs today and in the future. Charles Malik writes:

> *I really do not know what will remain of civilization and history if the accumulated influence of Christ, both direct and indirect, is eradicated from literature, art, practical dealings, moral standards, and creativeness in the different activities of mind and spirit.*

Indeed, how dark our world will be if men and women fail to let Jesus rule their hearts and nations. But how gloriously history will unfold when Jesus Christ is Lord of all!

So far we have seen how the unique birth, life, teachings, death, resurrection, and exaltation of Jesus prepared the way for our restoration to God and to our eternal destiny. But one final step remains—one that only you and I can take.

eight

"WHO DO YOU SAY I AM?"

PICTURE AGAIN WITH me the occasion when Jesus took His disciples away from the crowds to a deserted area where He could be alone for prayer.

After asking the disciples who others say He is, Jesus then asks them quietly, "Who do you say I am?"

And Peter replies confidently, "You are the Christ" (Mark 8:29).

If Jesus were to ask you, "Who do you say I am?" what would your answer be? Your response to this question will determine your eternal destiny—and the quality of life you can experience on this earth.

Considering the Evidence

I have yet to meet a person who has honestly considered the overwhelming evidence proving the deity of Jesus of Nazareth who does not admit that He is the Son of God. Yes, I have met some who do not believe that Jesus is the Son of

God. But as we have talked and reasoned together, they have been honest in confessing, "I have not taken the time to read the Bible or to consider the historical facts concerning Jesus."

Their rejection and sometimes resentment of Christ has inevitably been based upon a lack of knowledge, an unfortunate emotional experience, the inconsistency of some Christian, or perhaps the influence of a high school teacher or college professor; but always they have admitted that they have not honestly considered the person of Jesus Christ and His claims on their lives.

Some years ago, I was speaking to a group of students at the University of California in Los Angeles. Immediately following my address, I was approached by an angry young student, whom I later discovered was the leader of a radical group on campus.

"I resent your effort to convince these students to become Christians," he said. "You have no right to impose your views on them. You are older and more mature than they are, and they are like putty in your hands. I object to your trying to convert them into becoming Christians."

Of course, he had conveniently failed to acknowledge that his goal as leader of the radical group on campus was to do everything he could to influence the students to follow his way. But rather than argue, I invited him to our home for dinner. He agreed to come.

It was an interesting and delightful evening. We had a pleasant chat. I found him to be a personable young man, brilliant of mind and articulate. We had a good time together.

After we finished our meal, I thought it appropriate to talk to him about the Lord Jesus Christ. So I reached over and picked up my Bible. "I would like to read something to you from the Bible," I told him.

He reacted strongly. "I don't believe the Bible," he declared. "I don't want to hear anything you read. I've read the Bible from cover to cover, and it's filled with contradictions and myths. I don't believe a word of it!"

I responded calmly, "If you don't mind, I'll read a few portions anyway."

So I turned to the first chapter of the Gospel of John and read:

> *Before anything else existed, there was Christ, with God. He has always been alive and is himself God. He created everything there is—nothing*

exists that he didn't make. Eternal life is in him, and this life gives light to all mankind. His life is the light that shines through the darkness—and the darkness can never extinguish it (John 1:1–5, TLB).

I read several more verses and finished with:

Christ became a human being and lived here on earth among us and was full of loving forgiveness and truth. And some of us have seen his glory—the glory of the only Son of the heavenly Father (John 1:14, TLB).

"Let me see that," the young man said eagerly. "I don't think I've ever noticed that. I don't remember reading it." He went over the passage thoughtfully and handed the Bible back to me without comment.

Then I turned to Colossians 1 and read verses 13 through 20:

[God] has rescued us out of the darkness and gloom of Satan's kingdom and brought us into the Kingdom of his dear Son, who bought our freedom with his blood and forgave us all our sins.

Christ is the exact likeness of the unseen God. He existed before God made anything at all, and, in fact, Christ himself is the Creator who made everything in heaven and earth, the things we can see and the things we can't;...all were made by Christ for his own use and glory. He was before all else began and it is his power that holds everything together...

It was through what his Son did that God cleared a path for everything to come to him— all things in heaven and on earth—for Christ's death on the cross has made peace with God for all by his blood (TLB).

Again he asked if he could read the passage for himself. He appeared to read the verses over and over again because some time passed before he returned the Bible to me.

Then I turned to Hebrews 1 and read verses 1 through 3:

Long ago God spoke in many different ways to our fathers through the prophets..., telling them little by little about his plans.

But now in these days he has spoken to us through his Son to whom he has given everything, and through whom he made the world and everything there is.

God's Son shines out with God's glory, and all that God's Son is and does marks him as

God. He regulates the universe by the mighty power of his command. He is the one who died to cleanse us and clear our record of all sin, and then sat down in highest honor beside the great God of heaven (TLB).

By this time, the young man was obviously moved. His whole attitude of belligerence and antagonism was gone. So I turned to 1 John 2:22,23 and read:

Who is the greatest liar? The one who says that Jesus is not Christ. Such a person is antichrist, for he does not believe in God the Father and in his Son. For a person who doesn't believe in Christ, God's Son, can't have God the Father either. But he who has Christ, God's Son, has God the Father also (TLB).

When I finished reading, we chatted briefly. After awhile he stood and prepared to leave. I asked if he would write in our guest book. He nodded.

Following his name and address, he wrote these words, "The night of decision!" God's Holy Spirit had used the Word of God to break through his antagonism. Before my very eyes, the miracle had taken place. This young man had come face to face with the revolutionary, risen Son of God.

Your Invitation to Life

Have you discovered the joy and peace of personally placing your trust in Jesus Christ? Perhaps you have believed in the existence of God and His Son and have tried to live a good life but have never consciously invited Him to be your Savior and Lord.

No matter who you are—whether young or old, a professional or a student, married or single —at this very moment, you too can make the decision of a lifetime. Right now Jesus is knocking at the door of your heart. He offers you the same wonderful love and plan that hundreds of millions through the centuries have received with life-changing results. He has already paid the penalty for your sin. He is asking you, in the quiet of your heart, to yield your all to Him—your intellect, your will, your emotions.

The following four spiritual laws or principles (adapted from my booklet *The Four Spiritual Laws*) will help you discover how to know God personally and experience the abundant life He promises.

1. *God **loves** you and offers a wonderful **plan** for your life.*

God's Love

"God so loved the world that he gave his one and only Son, that whoever believes in him shall not perish but have eternal life" (John 3:16).

God's Plan

(Christ speaking:) "I came that they might have life, and might have it abundantly [that it might be full and meaningful]" (John 10:10).

Why is it that most people are not experiencing the abundant life? Because...

2. *Man is **sinful** and **separated** from God, so we cannot know and experience God's love and plan for our life.*

Man is Sinful

"All have sinned and fall short of the glory of God" (Romans 3:23).

We were all created to have fellowship with God, but because of our stubborn self-will, we chose to go our own independent way and fellowship with God was broken. This self-will, characterized by an attitude of active rebellion or passive indifference, is evidence of what the Bible calls sin.

Man is Separated

"The wages of sin is death [spiritual separation from God]" (Romans 6:23).

God is holy and man is sinful. A great gulf separates us from God because He cannot tolerate sin. People often try to achieve the abundant life through their own efforts, such as living a good life or devotion to philosophy or religion— but inevitably fail. The Bible clearly teaches that there is only one way to bridge this gulf:

3. *Jesus Christ is God's **only** provision for our sin. Through Him you can know and experience God's love and plan for your life.*

God's Word records three important facts to verify this principle:

Jesus Died in Our Place

"God demonstrates His own love toward us, in that while we were yet sinners, Christ died for us" (Romans 5:8).

Jesus Rose from the Dead

"Christ died for our sins...He was buried...He was raised on the third day, according to the Scriptures...He appeared to Peter, then to the twelve. After that He appeared to more than five hundred..." (1 Corinthians 15:3–6).

Jesus Is the Only Way to God

"Jesus said to him, 'I am the way, and the truth, and the life; no one comes to the Father but through Me'" (John 14:6).

Thus, God has taken the loving initiative to bridge the gulf that separates us from Him by sending His Son, Jesus Christ, to die on the cross in our place to pay the penalty for our sins. But it is not enough just to know these truths...

4. *We must individually **receive** Jesus Christ as Savior and Lord; then we can know and experience God's plan for our lives.*

We Must Receive Christ

"As many as received Him, to them He gave the right to become children of God, even to those who believe in His name" (John 1:12).

We Receive Christ through Faith

"By grace you have been saved through faith; and that not of yourselves, it is the gift of God; not as a result of works that no one should boast" (Ephesians 2:8,9).

When We Receive Christ, We Experience a New Birth

(Read John 3:1–8.)

We Receive Christ by Personal Invitation

(Christ is speaking:) "Behold, I stand at the door and knock; if anyone hears My voice and opens the door, I will come in to him" (Revelation 3:20).

Receiving Christ involves turning to God from self (repentance) and trusting Christ to come into our lives to forgive our sins and to make us the kind of people He wants us to be. Just to agree intellectually that Jesus Christ is the Son of God and that He died on the cross for our sins is not enough. Nor is it enough to have an emotional experience. We receive Jesus Christ by faith, as an act of the will.

These two circles represent two kinds of lives:

Self-Directed Life

S – Self is on the throne
† – Christ is outside the life
● – Interests are directed by self, often resulting in discord and frustration

Christ-Directed Life

† – Christ is in the life and on the throne
S – Self is yielding to Christ
● – Interests are directed by Christ, resulting in harmony with God's plan

Which circle best represents your life?

Which circle would you like to have represent your life?

You can receive Jesus Christ right now by faith through prayer. God knows your heart and is not so concerned with your words as He is with the attitude of your heart. Here is a suggested prayer that has helped millions of men and women around the world express faith in Him and invite Him into their lives:

> *Lord Jesus, I need You. Thank You for dying on the cross for my sins. I open the door of my life and receive You as my Savior and Lord. Thank You for forgiving my sins and giving me eternal life. Take control of the throne of my life. Make me the kind of person You want me to be.*

Experiencing the Life

If you truly believe that Jesus Christ is the Son of God, that He died on the cross for your sins and was raised from the dead, and if you sincerely turned your life over to Him, you have just received Jesus Christ as your personal Savior and Lord. You are now a child of God. Today you have begun to experience God's wonderful love and forgiveness.

By receiving Christ as Savior and Lord you are assured of everlasting life with Him in heaven:

> *He who has the Son has life; he who does not have the Son of God does not have life. I write these things to you who believe in the name of the Son of God so that you may know that you have eternal life (1 John 5:12,13).*

Once we have received Christ as Savior, we do not need to invite Him in again. He promises His followers, "I am with you always, even to the end of the world" (Matthew 28:20, TLB). His Holy Spirit will permanently dwell within us (2 Corinthians 1:22).

In summary, when you received Christ by faith, as an act of your will, many wonderful things happened including the following:

1. Christ came into your life (Revelation 3:20; Colossians 1:27).

2. Your sins were forgiven (Colossians 1:14).

3. You became a child of God (John 1:12).

4. You received eternal life (John 5:24).

5. You began the great adventure for which God created you (John 10:10, 2 Corinthians 5:17; 1 Thessalonians 5:18).

Can you think of anything more wonderful that could happen to you than receiving Christ? Take a moment right now to thank God in prayer for what He has done for you. By thanking Him, you demonstrate your faith.

Now that you have become a child of God, you will discover that the claims of history's greatest revolutionary are true for you today. To help you grow in your new life in Christ, I encourage you to study His Word—the Bible—and obey His commands. Go to Him daily in prayer, trusting Him for every detail of your life. As you do so, you will experience the abundant life He has promised. And as you faithfully worship and serve in a local church, you too will know the love and fellowship of other believers, the body of Christ. These principles have been used by God to enrich my life since I became a Christian in 1945.

Paul was so thrilled about Jesus that he exclaimed in Colossians 1:28, "Everywhere we go we talk about Christ to all who will listen" (TLB). I encourage you to experience the joy of helping others discover this exciting life for themselves as well. Share your faith in Christ with your friends, loved ones, and neighbors at every opportunity. Take the initiative to tell everyone you meet about the person and claims of our Lord Jesus Christ and the revolutionary way He can change their lives. This practice has been especially meaningful to me.

You too can be a part of the wonderful adventure of spreading His words and teachings everywhere you go throughout the world through your prayers, your finances, and your personal involvement. You can help others discover the true destiny for which they were created by introducing them to the Man who has no equal.

THE PROOF OF CHANGED LIVES

By Paul Eshleman

PEOPLE SOMETIMES say, "I guess you are really proud of what The JESUS Film Project has done." I always say that I don't think about it much because there is so much yet to do and so many people who have not yet heard, but I think we would be ungrateful to the Lord if we didn't stop and thank Him for all that He has already done. When we praise Him, we remember again who it was who did it. Certainly not us.

I would like to share with you a few stories of people who have encountered the risen Lord through the *"JESUS"* film. Some are small, some are big, but they are all blessings. They are evidence of the power of God; it is only Jesus Christ who has such an ability to change lives.

People don't always respond to Christ the first time they see the film. But because the film is based on Luke's Gospel, 70 percent of the script is taken directly from the Word of God, and the

Word of God does not return void.

In a very rural village on the island of Borneo, an 80-year-woman came forward at the end of the film to make a commitment to Christ. Her face was wrinkled and her skin paper-thin, but she had a radiant glow that could come only from having discovered at this advanced time in her life how she could live forever. Sometimes we talk about the great numbers of people who have come to know Christ through the *"JESUS"* film, but what it's all about is one person who finds out that she can know Jesus, that she can have eternal life because of what He did for her on the cross 2,000 years ago.

As the *"JESUS"* film continues to spread across the world, we hear incredible stories of what God seems to be doing in a supernatural way. In many Muslim countries, people are seeing visions in which Jesus appears to them and says, "I AM the way." They begin to seek how to know Him in a more personal way. In one village high in the mountains of Iran, people had heard that the way to know Jesus was to find the Book that tells about Him, which is the Bible. One night a man had a dream that if he went to a highway, there would be some men there who could give him a

Bible. So the next day, he made his way down the mountainside to the highway that ran through that area, sat on a rock and began to wait. Sometime later, two men who had just happened to pick up a shipment of Bibles that day from the border were driving along this highway. Suddenly, the steering on their car locked, and they couldn't budge the steering wheel more than an inch. They barely eased the car over to the side of the road, got out, put up the hood, and tried to figure out what was wrong with the steering. Suddenly this man, who had been sitting nearby, asked, "Are you the men with the Bibles?" Stunned that this man knew they had Bibles, they said, "Well, yes, we have Bibles," and he bought as many Bibles as he could, and made his way back to the village. The men with the Bibles then went back to see what was wrong with their car, and found that nothing was wrong, and they got in and drove away. No one can take any credit for what the Lord is doing supernaturally in so many parts of the world. We count it a privilege to serve Him with the *"JESUS"* film.

Sometimes in the distribution of the *"JESUS"* film throughout the world, people have paid the ultimate price. While we were recording the Iteso language for a tribe in Uganda, some of the cast returned to the village during a break in the recording. As they were leaving the city, a band of guerrilla fighters on the side of the road began to riddle their truck with automatic weapons fire. One of the men was shot through the head and was killed instantly, a little girl was shot in the leg, and the man who had played the part of Jesus, John Aluru, was shot through the heart. One of the tires was shot out, but the driver kept going anyway, driving over 1½ miles on just the tire rim to get away from the guerrilla fighters. They drove directly to a hospital where the little girl and John Aluru were taken to the emergency room. That night as John lay dying, our film technician, Abraham Kasika, went in to see him. John raised up in obvious deep pain and said, "Abraham, don't stop the dubbing. Uganda needs this film. I have done my part, but don't stop, and don't ever be afraid." The next morning John Aluru died. Today he's with the Lord, and I imagine that he is looking down over the battlements of heaven, because every time the Iteso film is shown in Uganda, it's the voice of John Aluru that is telling thousands of his own people how to know Christ as their Savior. Just in the very first showing of the film, in the high school where John was the principal, John's voice, playing the character of Jesus, helped scores of young men and women come to know Jesus in a personal way.

As our plane landed on a grass air strip in the Karamoja region of Northern Uganda, we were greeted by native tribesman with their spears. Because of fighting in the area, the Karamoja had had all of their cattle stolen, and 185,000 of them have died within the last year of starvation. We went to a field where there was a 6-foot-high hill of skulls, and I picked up two skulls, one in each hand. As I looked at them, I realized that six months earlier these people had been living human beings, and they just died of starvation. And as I held their skulls in my hands, I wondered whether they had ever had one opportunity to hear the message of Christ. I wondered how much people in this region knew about who Jesus really was. That afternoon we were in a little village, and I asked my interpreter, "Could we find out what people really know about Jesus?" So, we gathered about 15 individuals, and asked them one at a time, "Tell me, just what do you know about Jesus?" One by one they shook their heads and said, "I don't know him." "Where does he live?"

"No, I never heard of him." Finally, there was only one small 8-year-old boy left, and I said, "Ask him to tell me anything, anything at all he's ever heard about Jesus." A big tear ran down the little boy's face, and the interpreter said, "Sir, he would like to tell you about Jesus, but he has never, ever before heard his name." That day I thought, *I am only one person, but whatever I can do, I want to make sure there are no little boys or girls, men or women who don't get that one opportunity, that one chance to hear who Jesus really is.*

He is the only One who can change lives for all of eternity; He is the Man without equal.

RESOURCES

Transferable Concepts. This series of time-tested messages teaches the principles of abundant Christian life and ministry. These messages, available in book format and on video or audio cassette, include:

How You Can Be Sure You Are a Christian
How You Can Experience God's Love and
   Forgiveness
How You Can Be Filled with the Spirit
How You Can Walk in the Spirit
How You Can Be a Fruitful Witness
How You Can Introduce Others to Christ
How You Can Help Fulfill the Great Commission
How You Can Love by Faith
How You Can Pray with Confidence
How You Can Experience the Adventure of Giving
How You Can Study the Bible Effectively

A Great Adventure. Written as from one friend to another, this booklet (formerly the Van Dusen letter) explains how to know God personally and experience peace, joy, meaning, and fulfillment in life.

Have You Heard of the Four Spiritual Laws? One of the most effective and widely used evangelistic tools ever developed, the *Four Spiritual Laws* gives you a meaningful, easy-to-use way of sharing your faith with others.

Witnessing Without Fear. This best-selling, Gold Medallion book offers simple hands-on, step-by-step coaching on how to share your faith with confidence. The chapters give specific answers to questions people most often encounter in witnessing and provide a proven method for sharing your faith.

END NOTES

1. The *"JESUS"* film was sponsored and financed by Campus Crusade for Christ, produced and directed by John Heyman, and distributed by Warner Brothers. This film is a fulfillment of a dream God gave me as a new believer in 1945. Thirty-five years passed before it became a reality. In the first ten years after its completion, the film was viewed by nearly one-tenth of the world's population. As of 2003, the film has been translated into nearly eight hundred languages, and viewed by over five billion people in 236 countries.

2. Philip Schaff, *The Person of Christ* (New York: American Tract Society, 1913), p. 33. *The World Christian Encyclopedia*, edited by David Barrett, estimates the world's Christian population at 32.4 percent in 1985.

3. Schaff, *The Person of Christ*, pp. 137, 138.

4. Ibid.

5. The Pharisees were one of the three chief Jewish sects—the others being the Sadducees and the Essenes. The Pharisees were the strictest observers of the Law of Moses as well as Jewish religious traditions.

End Notes

6. Sherwood Eliot Wirt and Kersten Beckstrom, *Living Quotations for Christians* (New York: Harper & Row, Publishers, 1974), No. 1807.

7. Charles Malik, *Christ and Crisis* (Grand Rapids: William B. Eerdmans Publishing Company, 1962), pp. 67, 68, 70.

8. John Eldredge and Tom Hess, "Pro-life Heroes in a Hostile Age," *Citizen*, May 21, 1990, p. 11.

9. Alexander Roberts and James Donaldson, eds., *The Ante-Nicene Fathers* (Grand Rapids: William B. Eerdmans Publishing Company, 1973), p. 46.

10. John F. Walvoord, *Jesus Christ Our Lord* (Chicago: Moody Press, 1969), p. 22.

11. Michael Horton, ed., *The Agony of Deceit* (Chicago: Moody Press, 1990), p. 98.

12. Josephus, *The Works of Josephus* (Peabody, MA: Hendrickson Publishers, 1987), p. 480.

13. Merle D'Aubigne', D. D., *History of the Reformation* (Grand Rapids: Baker Book House, 1976), p. 42.

14. Frank S. Mead, ed., *The Encyclopedia of Religious Quotations* (Old Tappan, NJ: Fleming H. Revell Company, 1976), p. 90.

15. John Bartlett, *Familiar Quotations* (Boston: Little, Brown and Company, 1955), p. 618.

16. Mead, *Encyclopedia*, pp. 92, 93.

17. C. S. Lewis, *Surprised by Joy: The Shape of My Early Life* (New York: Harcourt and Brace, 1966), pp. 228, 229.

18. C. S. Lewis, *Mere Christianity* (New York: The MacMillan Company, 1960), pp. 40, 41.

19. Peter W. Stoner and Robert C. Newman, *Science Speaks* (Chicago: Moody Press, 1976), pp. 106–112.

20. Herbert Lockyer, *All the Messianic Prophecies of the Bible* (Grand Rapids: Zondervan Publishing House, 1973), p. 64.

21. Satan is pre-eminently "the Adversary." He is hostile to all goodness and is the chief opponent of God and man. He aims to undo the work of God and seeks to persuade men to sin.

22. Herbert Lockyer, *All the Doctrines of the Bible* (Grand Rapids: Zondervan Publishing House, 1964), p. 40.

23. Finis Jennings Dake, *God's Plan for Man* (Lawrenceville, GA: Dake Bible Sales, Inc., 1949), pp. 372, 373.

24. Sherwood Eliot Wirt and Kersten Beckstrom, *Living Quotations for Christians* (New York: Harper & Row, Publishers, 1974), No. 1749.

25. My wife, Vonette, while chairman of the National Day of Prayer, lobbied both houses of Congress to declare the first Thursday of every May as the official National Day of Prayer. The vote was unanimous and signed into law by President Ronald Reagan. She also worked with both Presidents Reagan and George Bush who called for a return to prayer and Bible reading in the schools.

William R. Bright

Founder, Chairman, and President Emeritus,
Campus Crusade for Christ International

From a small beginning in 1951, the organization he began now has a presence in 196 countries in areas representing 99.6% of the world's population. Campus Crusade for Christ has more than 70 ministries and major projects, utilizing more than 25,000 full-time and 500,000 trained volunteer staff. Each ministry is designed to help fulfill the Great Commission, Christ's command to help carry the gospel of God's love and forgiveness in Christ to every person on earth.

Born in Coweta, Oklahoma, on October 19, 1921, Bright graduated with honors from Northeastern State University, and completed five years of graduate study at Princeton and Fuller Theological Seminaries. He holds five honorary doctorates from prestigious institutions and has received numerous other recognitions, including the ECPA Gold Medallion Lifetime Achievement Award (2001), the Golden Angel Award as International Churchman of the Year (1982), and the $1.1 million Templeton Prize for Progress in Religion (1996), which he dedicated to promoting fasting and prayer throughout the world.

He has received the first-ever Lifetime Achievement Award from his alma mater (2001).

Bright has authored more than 100 books, booklets, videos and audio tapes, as well as thousands of articles and pamphlets, some of which have been printed in most major languages and distributed by the millions. Among his books are: *Come Help Change the World, The Secret, The Holy Spirit, A Man Without Equal, A Life Without Equal, The Coming Revival, The Transforming Power of Fasting & Prayer, Red Sky in the Morning* (co-author), *GOD: Discover His Character, Living Supernaturally in Christ,* and the booklet *Have You Heard of the Four Spiritual Laws?* (which has an estimated 2.5 billion circulation).

He has also been responsible for many individual initiatives in ministry, particularly in evangelism. For example, the *"JESUS"* film, which he conceived and financed through Campus Crusade, has, by latest estimates, been viewed by over 4.6 billion people in 236 nations and provinces.

Bright and his wife, Vonette, who assisted him in founding Campus Crusade for Christ, live in Orlando, Florida. Their two sons, Zac and Brad, and their wives, Terry and Katherine, are also in full-time Christian ministry.